"It is a sad day when a woman loses her power, because when you lose your power, you lose *yourself*."

CU

Woman Find Thyself

CATHY UPSHIRE

WOMAN FIND THYSELF

Woman Find Thyself
Copyright © 2017 by Cathy Upshire

Published by Inscribe United Press Publishing Co.

Cover Design: Cathy Upshire
Interior Design: Cathy Upshire

ISBN-13: 978-0989154314 (Inscribe United Press Publishing Co.)
ISBN-10: 0989154319

All rights reserved. No part of this publication may be reproduced, stored in or introduced into a retrieval system, or transmitted in any form or by any means (electronic, mechanical, photocopying, recording or otherwise), without the prior written permission of the above publisher of this book.

Library of Congress Cataloging-in-Publication Data

Printed in the United States of America

WOMAN FIND THYSELF

This book is dedicated to:

My children
Andre, Quincy and Aja
Three beautiful gifts from God.

and

My late mom, Leathia Morris.
Mom, I present Woman Find Thyself
as an offering to women everywhere
in honor of you.

WOMAN FIND THYSELF

This is book is not complete; it's a work in progress. Why? Because *I'm* a work in progress. Just when I thought I had arrived at my journey's destination, there was something new to learn and explore, not only about myself, but the world around me and how I was going to navigate my way through it. Do I speak or keep quiet; walk away or stay? Do I throw my hands up and quit or lean in and drudge forward? Sometimes I know *exactly* what to do; sometimes not. Just as our bodies are changing on a cellular level every day, so are we on a spiritual level. My physical body isn't the same body it was ten years ago, neither am I (the woman who lives within me). She's stronger, she's wiser, she's healed; she's whole. But there's still yet more to experience and learn; to explore and overcome. But I am going to share with you what I've learned and what I know thus far, and use what I've learned to help you get started on your personal journey; the journey to wholeness, healing, and authenticity.

Enjoy

Woman Find Thyself

My Manifesto

I woke up this morning rejoicing in the God of my salvation for what great things he has done. Things that can't be measured, bought or seen with the naked eye; things that let me know He's still working. I thank my God, because He took the shackles off my feet so I could dance. And so I will.

I declare and decree that I will come out of the shadows and allow the "Son" to shine upon my countenance and use me as he will. I will not allow fear, self-doubt or uncertainty to inhibit me from walking boldly into my purpose, because I understand that there are many who are waiting on me to make a contribution to their lives. I commit that wherever I go 'I' will show up. Not someone I think the people around me are more apt to embrace or endorse. No. Just me—me and my Authentic Self.

I will make no attempts whatsoever for the sake of anyone to modify or tamper with the tapestry and mastery of God's handiwork, for I am fearfully and wonderfully made. Simply put? I declare from this day forward . . . I will be ME.

Woman Find Thyself

Table of Contents

FORWARD..15
MANDATE 21
THE DANGERS OF ASSUMING THE ROLE OF VICTIM.......25
THE LESSON 29
FINDING CATHY..31
ENFORCING BOUNDARIES 35
THE LESSON 41
PRE-EXISTING WOUNDS 43
THE LESSON 47
THE OATH OF TRUTH 49
WHAT ROLE DID YOU PLAY IN THE MESS 51
EXERCISE 55
IDENTITY THEFT 57
WANTED 61
EXERCISE 63
EPIPHANY 65
EVIDENCE OF FOUL PLAY..69
EXERCISE 71
HAVE YOU SEEN ME?..73
EXERCISE 75

MISSING	77
MISSING PERSONS REPORT	79
EXERCISE	81
CAPTAIN OF MY SOUL	83
PERSONAL CONSENT FORM	87
POWER BOOSTERS	89
It is a sad day	91
Emotional pain and woundedness	93
Show me a woman	95
People aren't necessary causing your pain	97
Instead of trying to be yourself	99
Shame isn't about others' perception	101
There's nothing worse	103
I want people to love me	105
When we accept and embrace who we are	107
Rejection is a feeling	109
Neediness and personal power	111
When we give away our power	113
Wholeness is being able to be	115
You can't look to those who hurt you	117
What you're feeling on the inside	119
No—You Think She Is	121

If someone has a negative opinion of you 123
You're not going to think to change yourself........125
The issue is not that others don't accept you.........127
Better to be disliked for being who you are 129
If you don't like someone 131
To avoid making the same mistake.......................133
A scar is a permanent record 135
There is a lesson, a treasure, a connection.............137
You will find if you haven't already 139
Wholeness is not needing anything.......................141

RHYTHM OF MY HEART 143
Why Am I Here?..145
Broken Wing..147
Had a Great Fall 149
And So I Hide...151
I Lift Up My Head...153
Hole in My Soul..155
I Thirst..157
Looking for Love 159
Can You See Me?..161
Prisoner to a Fortified Heart........................... 163
Face to Face 165

The Imposter.......... 167
What Would You Do 169
Beauty That Really Matters 171
I Thought I Knew 173
Starting Over 175
What's in Your Box 177
Loving the Woman Within 179
Authentic Woman 181
Satisfied 183

WOMAN FIND THYSELF

Woman Find Thyself

FORWARD

By Stephanie Harrison

In October of 2016 I met and opened my arms to Cathy Upshire and my heart soon followed. I love connecting with women who are on a mission to empower others to walk in their purpose.

It is my life's greatest joy as a pastor, wife, sister, daughter, mother of four, and spiritual mom to many, to be a "thumbprint", if you will, to cultivate, protect, and guide the DNA assigned to every individual. You have DNA that is unique to you and so do I. I have fought for mine. Some of that fight meant kicking down boxes others had created for me and tearing down walls; walls I'd built around myself. And sometimes it meant finding the courage to peel back the many layers of myself to find the little girl I wasn't even aware I'd lost.

There is nothing in this world more beautiful than embracing your path and being an eye witness to the purpose of God being carried out in the lives of others.

I'm sure every woman can attest to the fact that the struggle we all have to cling to the little girl we once knew before life made its imprint on us is a never ending process. Life and the circumstances we encounter have a way of altering our identities over time; changing who we are at our very core without our permission to do so.

There is something liberating about a woman who has lived many lives, walking through the fire and then coming out with a boldness to tell her story. Cathy's story is one whose plot went from victim to *Victor!* She so courageously opens up her heart in the pages of this book to gives tangible insights and practical ways for women who are in the middle of an identity crisis to find themselves. And *you* are *in there!* You are worth putting in the work to find *yourself*.

Cathy is committed in her ministry to women. Her heart for you will leap off of the pages of this book as she loves you back to *life*. Don't live one more day lost in the shadows of your present existence. You are an *Overcomer!* You are *Enough! Find* Thyself.

As you open this book I pray that God opens your heart to the process of being found.

ಖ ಖ ಖಖ ಖ ಖ

Stephanie Harrison is the Co-Pastor of The Kingdom Center Church in Louisville, KY. She is also the Founder of UnBecomingMe.com; The Unbecoming Movement; a movement that's empowering women everywhere to "Unbecome" other's expectations of them so that they can find their own voice and their way back to who God originally intended them to be.

WOMAN FIND THYSELF

Beauty for my Ashes

Isaiah 61:3

WOMAN FIND THYSELF

Mandate

Holy Spirit led me into the *Wilderness* with a mandate to abandon my personal power and true identity to assume, in my estimate, one of the most ignominious of roles—that of a victim. Holy Spirit didn't use the word "victim" per se. His words? *"I don't want you to fight anymore battles."* This was especially challenging for me, because my ability to stand up for myself allowed me to set boundaries that protected me from malicious intent. And my boundaries, I might add, were *well* established. People knew how far they could go and went no further. *"If you're willing and obedient,"* Holy Spirit went on. *"I will use the pain."* Use the pain? Hearing him say, use the pain was a bit unsettling, to say the least, because it meant something really bad was coming, and *boy* was I right. And *then* he said, *"Don't tell anyone about this exchange."* Now—*that* was a hard pill to swallow. It was bad enough he didn't want me to stand up for myself, but not being able to tell anybody why wasn't something I was willing to sign up for.

Over the weeks that followed I kept thinking about what Holy Spirit said, *"If you're willing and obedient, I will use the pain."* Those words kept going off in my head like a siren, *"I will use the pain...I will use the pain...I will use the pain."* I *wanted* Holy Spirit to use me; more than *anything*. So as scared as I was—and when I tell you I was scared I was SCARED!—I surrendered to the call.

Fast forward several decades.

Woman Find Thyself

Woman Find Thyself

THE DANGERS OF ASSUMING THE ROLE OF VICTIM

I was a good Christian woman (26 years old) who obeyed all the rules; no pants, no earrings, no red shoes. And as far back as I can remember, even as far back as the third grade, I was afraid of God; afraid of his power and what he'd do if I disobeyed. So when I felt the call to let him *"fight my battles"*, unfortunately, I took it to the extreme.

My husband was a violent man and a repository for rage. My efforts to defuse his anger proved futile. So I did what I thought a good Christian woman *should* do; I gave it to God. And *that* was where it all began. I gave God a battle he had intended for *me* to fight. And the role I played in my marriage from that day on was that of "the victim".

I've been around a long time and I've learned many things; some I'd just soon forget. But if I had to choose just one piece of advice to give to a young woman, it would be this...don't *ever* allow yourself to become a victim, because a victim is a woman with no power. And I'm going to share with you what I've learned about the dangers of assuming such a powerless role.

I learned that the more I allowed myself to *be* a victim the more victimized I became. It was as if I had a neon sign on my back that read, "Can't kick the dog? Kick me!" And since I had assumed the role *of* a victim, over time I started talking like one, I started walking like one, I started thinking like one. And as time went on I started looking like one; all of which opened the door to a myriad of unhealthy behaviors that had a negative impact on my relationship with family and friends.

However, what I never saw coming when I accepted this powerless role was the total desecration of my view of *myself* and the waning of my self-worth. And because I starting feeling within myself I had no worth (which I hadn't experienced before) I started seeking it through external means. On a subconscious level I thought, perhaps, if I gained the acceptance and approval of the right people, those associations would give me a greater sense of my own worth. However, seeking other people's acceptance and approval only lead to a boat load of rejection; which left me not only dealing with the *sting* of rejection, but feeling much like damaged goods; like I had a manufacturer's defect of sorts.

It wasn't long before I started isolating myself, not only physically, but emotionally as well. I had a wall up so thick it was virtually impenetrable. Consequently, no one could see my value if they *wanted* to let alone my true worth. Since no one could see it, so I thought, I set out to prove I had it. So I started living a performance driven life. I thought maybe if I did something great, people would think I *was* great. That seemed to work a little, but the problem with that was I had to keep going from one great thing to the next. That was *exhausting!* There I was...educated, doing farely well, multi-talented, and kinda cute. I mean—I had the goods.

By all appearances it looked like I had it all together, but on the inside I was a hot molten *mess!* For years I allowed myself to be mistreated and maltreated, misused and abused. I suffered from depression, shame, social anxiety, a loss of identity, a drawback spirit, an intense fear of rejection; of being abandoned, and on occasion, thoughts of suicide. A mess I was until one day Holy Spirit said it was FINISHED and that I shall be a victim no more.

Once I stopped playing "the victim" I felt almost immediately the fierceness of the personal power I had previously possessed. It was as if I clicked my heels and there it was—*Power*—power to set boundaries and draw my own personal lines. And I've been drawing them every since and you can too.

THE LESSON

If life as a victim has taught me anything, it has taught me this—not the least of which is—when you assume the role of victim in one relationship you're, unwittingly, laying the ground work to be victimized in another; not only by another significant other, but by people in general, because the energy and the vibrational frequencies you're projecting to the world and the people around you spell "V-I-C-T-I-M". And as a result, you become a sitting target for those who can't kick their dogs. And it takes a lot of hard work to reverse that signature; a feat to which some never achieve.

Woman Find Thyself

FINDING CATHY

You are sent into the Wilderness for one reason, and one reason only: Woman, find thyself.

SARAH BAN BREATHNACH

My journey didn't begin with a hunger to be healed though I needed it. I yearned to be whole. And I knew if I stood any chance of becoming whole, I had to find *me*; that part of me who got lost on some strange stretch of road; who I hadn't seen since; who I'd written off as a missing person stored in a cold case file in a dark alcove of my heart. But I realized somewhere along the way that if I could just find her—me, the *real* me—my wounds would be healed and once again I'd be whole. Because the woman I'd lost on that stretch of road was *already* whole. She knew nothing of fear and anxiety, low self-esteem and low self-worth. And victim?—No way; not to a woman *or* a man, because she would never have assumed such a powerless role. She was authentic; she was gutsy; she was powerful, she was *A FORCE*. And I knew if I could just find her and allow myself to become enmeshed in her again, she'd be my saving grace. And *that's* where my journey began. I didn't know where my journey was going to take me or how treacherous the terrain, but I geared up. Was I going to be able to find her? Honestly, I didn't know. But like Tom Hanks in "Saving Private Ryan", I was going to die trying.

Woman Find Thyself

Woman Find Thyself

Enforcing Boundaries

*If there are no consequences,
the behavior will persist.*

- Dr. Phil McGraw

People tend to respect boundaries; not only because they've been set, but because they're being enforced. If I put a fence up around my house, people will—for the most part—respect my space. They're not going to jump over my fence or camp out on my lawn. And if someone does, I assure you there will be consequences. It may be something as simple as me running out of the house wielding a big stick yelling, "*Get off of my lawn!*" or something as drastic as calling the police. But there would be a reaction; one that would cause the trespasser to think twice about doing it again. And I'm sure the trespasser would get a reaction out of you as well. Maybe not the same reaction, but a reaction just the same.

If we wouldn't give a second thought to running out of our houses wielding a big stick or calling the police to ward off someone who's taken the liberty to pitch a tent out on our lawns, why wouldn't we respond in a way that would ward off someone who's ignoring the boundaries we've set for ourselves (presuming we've set some).

Yes—setting boundaries is a must, but as you can see it's not enough. We must have the courage to impose consequences when those boundaries are being violated or ignored. If we don't, unacceptable behaviors from those who are ruthless, callus and cruel will persist.

But the question is…why *don't* we set boundaries; why don't we draw lines. I have found that the reason we don't have the courage to do so is because we don't want to rock the boat or tip it over. Well let me tell you—when you start putting your foot down stuff is going to hit the fans and you're going to have to be okay with it for a season. As Depak Chopra, a two times New York Times bestselling author and global pioneer in the field of mind/body medicine said, *"Every great change is preceded by Chaos"*. It may get a little chaotic for a while, but you're going to have to weather the storm. Change starts with *YOU*.

Because I am a Christian woman I have to address the issue of Love. We are given the mandate to love our neighbor as ourselves. But love is not always nice. And those two words (love and nice) aren't interchangeable. If you don't believe me ask the people who were in the Temple when Jesus turned over the tables of the money exchangers. That was a classic example of love not being nice. He loved them, but a boundary had been crossed and it was important that they saw a "demonstration" of his displeasure (a consequence).

I can't think of a greater love than the love a mother has for her child. But her interactions with them aren't always so nice. When my children were little I did some things that, if you asked them, weren't so nice; a spanking here, a grounding there. But I had the awesome responsibility of teaching them boundaries; teaching them how to behave appropriately whether it was towards me or someone else.

We teach people how to treat us. If our aim is to show love, were going to have to be prepared to show the other side of that coin; the tough side. There's a scripture in the Bible that say, there is a time for everything…there's a time for peace and then there's a time for war." We're not talking a fist fight, but you get the point. Don't get caught in the "nice" trap or let someone tell you if you're not being nice, you're not showing love. I spent many, many years being nice; hoping if I was nice enough, I'd get the love and respect I so desired and I got *nothing*; nothing but more of what I didn't want.

One of the greatest pieces of advice I was given as a young woman was given to me by my cousin, friend and confidante, Joyce Tucker. She said, "Cathy, when you change the people around you will change." It was the best advice I'd ever received, but it was the advice it took the longest to execute and believe. I just couldn't comprehend that something so simple could be so true. But 15 years after I received that advice I learned it *was* true. You can invite crazy into your life (and I did) and you can usher it out (did that too). The change you want to see starts with *YOU*.

It's time to STOP the madness. Learn how to confront those who are violating your boundaries. If you can't do it face to face, send a video. If you can't do that, send an audio recording. If you can't do that, send an email or a text message. If you can't do that, write a letter. But for God's sake, do *SOMETHING!* Find a way to let those who are violating your boundaries know that their behavior is NOT acceptable.

By the way, say those words out loud right now, *"That is NOT acceptable".* Emphasize the word "Not". Say it again. In fact, practice saying it over and over again. I said it to someone shaking in my booths, but it did the job and I didn't lose one ounce of their love. In fact, they loved me the more AND I gained a greater level of their respect.

Someone is reading this right now and you know *exactly* what I'm talking about. You're being treated in ways that are totally unacceptable. But instead of confronting the person about their behavior, you shrink and cower down. You're afraid that if you do confront them, your actions are going to sever the relationship and you'll be abandoned or dropped. *That* was a biggie for me. But I decided I'd rather be a happy hermit than a tormented soul.

The Lesson

If you live your life playing the victim or "the wounded one", you may get people to feel sorry for you (a victim's modus operandi), but you're *not* going to get anyone to stay off your lawn. Without boundaries (coupled with consequences), people are going to treat you however they want and they will continue to until you come to the same resolve as Peter Finch in the 1976 movie classic "Network" when he yelled out of an office building window, *"I am mad as hell and I'm not gonna TAKE IT anymore!"*

Woman Find Thyself

PRE-EXISTING WOUNDS

I'd organized a women's event to speak to the women about the impact pre-existing wounds have on our lives. To drive home the point I wrapped my left arm in a make shift sling, symbolizing a hidden injury, then called one of the women (we'll call her Gloria) to the front of the room. I instructed Gloria to walk towards me on my right side—bumping into my right arm as she passes by. For the sake of this illustration, let's say the sling was under my sweater and out of view. This is how it played out.

Gloria: Bumps into my arm. "Oh—I'm sorry!"
Me: "Oh! It's okay, I'm fine."

THE END

Then I instructed Gloria to repeat the same scenario on my left side.

Gloria walks towards me accidentally bumping into my left arm; which as you recall was in a sling.

Gloria: Bumps into my arm. "Oh—I'm sorry!"

Me: "Oh my God!!!" I screeched in agony! "Oh my Go—d!!! My Arm!!!

Gloria: "Oh! I'm sorry! Are you okay?!"

Me: Doubled over in pain; going from one end of the stage to the other. "My arm!! My arm!! Oh my God!!! My arm!" After a minute or so I ran into the audience telling some of the woman what Gloria did and how badly she hurt me; totally vilifying her and assassinating her character.

Gloria: Stands there befuddled, because she knew she hadn't bumped me hard enough to cause any pain.

THE END

After the drama had ended I asked the women, "In your estimate did Gloria do anything wrong?" The consensus in the room was a resounding "NO!" Even they could see the absurdity of what had transpired. Gloria hadn't done anything other than what she'd done to my right arm; which didn't bother me at all. But because my left arm had an injury that hadn't healed (a pre-existing condition) what Gloria did, accidentally or not, triggered unfathomable pain.

This dramatization illustrates how hyper-sensitive we become when we have pre-existing conditions or wounds that have not healed. Things that wouldn't *normally* hurt us do. A simple bump on the arm wouldn't normally hurt *anybody*, but it would if the arm was fractured or broke.

When I began to reflect back over some of the painfully episodic episodes of *my* past from a whole and healed place, I got confused. I kept thinking over and over again, "Why the heck did *that* hurt?" Even *I* could see the absurdity of some of the things that caused me pain. I could clearly see that much of the pain I'd been carrying around for all those years was simply a result of ancient wounds that hadn't healed;

making me hyper-sensitive to everything. I mean—*everything* hurt; even things that shouldn't have.

THE LESSON

Much of the emotional pain you're experiencing has little to do with what someone did and more to do with the condition of your arm.

Woman Find Thyself

THE OATH OF TRUTH

*The naked truth is always better
than the best dressed lie.*

--Ann Landers

With my left hand over my heart
and my right hand raised...

I do solemnly promise
to tell myself the truth,
the whole truth,
and nothing *but* the truth
so help me God.

Woman Find Thyself

WHAT ROLE DID YOU PLAY IN THE MESS

My journey to wholeness began with the truth—the *ugly* truth, and when I tell you it was ugly, it was *uuu-gly*. So ugly I turned away. *No—I am not that person! I did NOT play a role in that mess!* Of course, I didn't say those words verbally or out loud, but my spirit was bellowing it at the top of its lungs.

It is so easy to blame others for the pain and messes in our lives. I think we've all been guilty of it to some degree. But the role we may have played may not have been that we did something wrong; it may have been what we didn't do. And that may have played just as much a role in the mess as what the other person involved did.

We tend to vilify those who hurt us (present company included). If we can vilify or blame someone else, we can come out looking squeaky clean. *"Oh the holiness of being the injured party."* Maya Angelo shares in her exquisite book *Singin' and Swing' and Getting' Merry Like Christmas.* But I knew if I continued to blame others for my lingering pain, I'd never find my way back to being me—to being whole. And my hunger to be whole outweighed whose fault it was, who started it or who should pay. All I wanted was to be whole again and I didn't care who was to blame; even if the person who got blamed was me. So to start I took my focus off of everyone else and focused "solely" on me, because it really was about me. I started eradicating words like, "he, she, they and them" from my vocabulary. I call them the vocabulary of a victim—a role I was no longer willing to play. And thus my journey began and it started with one word—"I".

I started thinking about what *I* did, what *I* put up with, what *I* allowed. I focused on what *I* did to *myself.* I realized the greatest perpetrator against me *was* me.

But what was so astonishing was the level of power I felt rising in me when I started using the word "I". I discovered it was such a liberating word. It gave me a sense of restored dignity. I felt less a victim and more of a woman who was taking control of herself; of her *life*.

Woman Find Thyself

EXERCISE

What are *you* blaming other people for? List them below. Now write down the role *you* played in the mess. Tell yourself the *Truth*, because the truth will set you free.

___
___
___
___
___
___
___
___
___
___
___
___
___
___
___
___

Woman Find Thyself

IDENTITY THEFT

Have you found yourself engaging in behaviors that are out of character for you lately; like seeking other peoples' approval; even worse, trying to win their love? Are you allowing yourself to be treated in ways you said, *emphatically*, you'd never allow? Have you been in situations where you've caught yourself trying to prove your value and your worth? And what about your power; your personal power? Are you starting to behave more and more like a helpless victim than that of the fierce, powerful, confident woman you really are? If you answered yes to any of the above, you may have been a victim of Identity Theft. The culprit? An "Imposter"; a fugitive who has evaded the law; who's "wanted" for stealing the identities of millions of unsuspecting women, and she will stop at nothing to steal yours.

She has no name or identity of her own. She takes on the identity of those who will let her and then morphs into a woman her victims barely recognize. And some of you already know where this woman is, because she's living in your house. You see her every time you look in the mirror. She looks like you, she talks like you, she walks like you, but you know deep down inside this woman isn't you.

If this woman is living in your house, robbing you of your power and true identity, you're going to have to confront her and have her removed. If you don't, she's going to transform herself into someone you're not going to like very much and may even grow to detest and loathe, because she will have wreaked *havoc* in your life. And you will regret the day you set idly by and allowed her to run amuck.

Woman Find Thyself

Woman Find Thyself

WOMAN FIND THYSELF

WANTED

An Imposter

Guilty of the following Crimes

Giving away my power and self-respect
Allowing others to impose their own expectations on her
Failing to set boundaries & impose consequences
Seeking other people's acceptance and approval
Trying to prove her value and her worth
Being overly accommodating
People pleasing
Playing the role of victim
Failing to live authentically
Putting herself at the bottom of the list or not on it at all

WOMAN FIND THYSELF

EXERCISE

What crimes is the woman in *your* mirror guilty of committing again you? List them below.

_____
_____
_____
_____
_____
_____
_____
_____
_____
_____
_____
_____
_____
_____
_____
_____
_____
_____

Woman Find Thyself

Epiphany

I'd been invited to a prayer breakfast to do some dramatized interpretations of my poetry from my Evolution of a Woman collection. There were several poems I wanted to do, but I decided on "The Imposter" and "Face to Face". I'd done them many times before, but not as a "published" work. So I was especially excited about that. I had somewhere in the neighborhood of 50-60 books left over from a previous engagement, so I figured I had more than enough.

The event organizer introduced me and called me to the platform to share my presentations. I did Face-to-Face first and ended with The Imposter. Surges of laughter rose and fell with spontaneous applause. The energy in the room was electrifying.

I was delighted to see that the women had enjoyed the presentations as they always do, but before I left the podium I mentioned that Evolution of a Woman was available for purchase at the table in the back of the room.

I took my seat at the table that had been reserved for the prayer breakfast organizer and her special guests as the speaker made her way to the front. I was sitting there preparing my heart to receive "The Word" when a woman came from behind and stooped down beside my chair. "Excuse me." She whispered. "Can you sign my book?" I felt a little uncomfortable, because the speaker had just gotten up to speak, and signing books while the speaker was up didn't seem like an appropriate thing to do.

"Are you gonna be here after the breakfast?" I whispered back.

"Yes, but you're gonna be swamped." *Swamped!* What did she mean by that? It totally did not compute. But what left me standing with my mouth open was what happened after the benediction. I looked over towards the back of the room and noticed that my daughter, who was responsible for book sales, had cleared the table. Everything had been boxed up and put away. I rushed over to see why she'd do such a thing.

"Aja! What are you doing?" I fussed. "Somebody might want a book!"

"Momma!" Aja jumped in. "Those books are gone!" I just stood there, mouth opened, transfixed.

"What do you mean gone!"

"They're all gone. The women just kept coming to get'em."

"While the message was going on?"

"Yeah!"

And the women were *still* coming. It was in that moment I realized we all had to some degree an imposter who needed to be dealt with and removed. Mine had already been, but the residue of her scent still lingered and I wasn't stopping until I was convinced there was no trace of her having been there at all. And so my journey continued.

Woman Find Thyself

Evidence of Foul Play

Let's just say for a moment you have an imposter living in *your* house and you want to have her removed. The first thing you're going to have to do is contact the authorities (we're pretending of course). Unfortunately, they're not going to be able to do anything without a search warrant and they can't obtain one without probable cause. So you're going to have to provide evidence to substantiate you claim that the woman living in your house is indeed an imposter.

What evidence can you give the authorities to prove that the woman living in your house is an imposter; that she really isn't you? In other words, what exactly is this woman doing that is totally out of character for you? Make a list. If you need help, ask a close friend; a loved one; someone you trust to help you get to the bottom of the matter. Demand the truth. I selected five people I loved and trusted; people who had no interest in hurting me with the truth; who saw the good in me and loved me in spite of the bad. I asked one simple question. What kinds of things am I doing that seem totally out of character for me; things you didn't think you'd every see me do? What areas do I need to work on? I told everyone if they didn't come up with *something*, I was going to be very disappointed. It was difficult for them to tell me the truth for fear of hurting my feelings, but they did. They all came up with *something*.

The more I probed the more I learned and the more I learned the more I started remembering, *Yeah! I would never have done that!...I would never have said that!...I would never have tolerated that!* It was an eye opening experience and it was extremely helpful in my pursuit of finding my way back to me.

Exercise

What evidence do you have that the woman in your mirror is an imposter; that this woman isn't you.

Woman Find Thyself

HAVE YOU SEEN ME?

When I started my journey to finding me—the *real* me—I realized almost immediately I was going to need help with this one too, because the real me had been gone for so long I didn't know who the real me was. I couldn't remember how she laughed, how she interacted with people, how she entered a room, how she navigated her way in the world period. I couldn't remember anything. I'd become so many different people—trying to be liked—I lost sight of who *I* was. I wanted so badly to be me, but I couldn't remember who *me* was. So I created what amounted to a Missing Persons Report. I started soliciting family members and those who knew me "back-in-the-day" for information, asking them what they remembered about me—especially before I got married. I started there, because that was where the real me was last seen; the decade where I felt more my true self.

I learned a lot from this exercise. It started me to remembering again and connecting the dots. But what I really loved about it was hearing all of the *good* things people saw in me as a young woman; things I had no idea they saw. This exercise helped me tremendously.

Exercise

For the sake of this exercise I want you to personify your authentic self. In other words imagine she's a real person and that she's gone missing. Then image you've gone to the police station to report her missing. One of the first things they're going to tell you to do is fill out a Missing Persons Report; describing the person who's gone missing; in which case would be your authentic self. How would you describe her so that someone else would be able to identify her if they saw her? And what about your posters? Besides having a picture of you on it, what would it say? Here's the poster I created for my missing person on the next page. I couldn't find a picture of me in my twenties (not one I liked), so I just grabbed something I thought was cute. But you'll get the jist.

Woman Find Thyself

WOMAN FIND THYSELF

MISSING

My Authentic Self

Last Seen: Decades Ago
Name: Cathy Upshire
Height: 5' 3"; Weight: 126 lbs
Hair Color: Black
Eyes Color: Hazel Brown
Boundaries: Several

Self Esteem: High
Self-Confidence: High
Self-Worth: High
Personal Power: High
Fear of Rejection: None
Playing the Victim: Never

If you have any information or remember *anything* about my authentic self, please *Say Something*. Any information you provide may help me find my way back to me.

Woman Find Thyself

WOMAN FIND THYSELF

Missing Persons Report

Have You Seen Me

Name of missing person:
Cathy Upshire

Relationship to person filing report:
My Authentic Self

When did you last see her?
Several Decades Ago

DESCRIPTION OF MISSING PERSON

Please provide a description of the missing person. Provide as many details as possible.

1. What were her personality traits?
2. What made her unique (a uniqueness that existed before the age of sixteen?
3. What boundaries had she set for herself?
4. How did she respond when those boundaries were being violated?
5. How did she demonstrate personal power?
6. What was her opinion or view of herself?
7. What was she passionate about?
8. What made her feel most alive?
9. What types of things did she enjoy doing?
10. What were her aspirations and dreams?
11. What kinds of things did she do for herself?
12. Is there anything else you can tell us about your authentic self? If so, please list them below
13. _____
14. _____
15. _____

Woman Find Thyself

EXERCISE

Those were some of the questions I asked myself. How would you answer those questions if the person you knew yourself to be went missing?

_____
_____
_____
_____
_____
_____
_____
_____
_____
_____
_____
_____
_____
_____
_____
_____
_____
_____

WOMAN FIND THYSELF

CAPTAIN OF MY SOUL

"It matters not how straight the gate,
How charged with punishments the scroll,
I am the master of my fate;
the captain of my soul."

--William Ernest Henley

For many years my spirit was in a tumultuous state of utter unrest for reasons I could neither account for nor explain, but somehow I managed to keep living what I considered to be the hand I'd been dealt. But one day during a moment of quiet introspection I had an epiphany; an awakening of sorts. I realized that the life I had been living wasn't my life at all. It was the life the people around me had created for themselves. I had simply enmeshed myself into *their* lives instead of living a life of my own.

But *peace and contentment came* when I began to create a life of my own and of my own doing, when I began to invite others to share in my life as opposed to just tagging along in theirs, when I realized life didn't stop with any one person or any one event; and that I could live—I mean *really* live—whether someone was a participant in my life or not; and that those who chose to leave could leave; and I could let them leave even without malice; because I was no longer looking through the window of *their* Thomas Kinkade homes; hoping they'd invite me in, but that I was on the inside of my *own* home, my own life, with a welcome sign on the door that read "You're Welcomed; Come on In." Allowing those who'd come in to stay as long as they wanted and allowing them to leave when they decided it was time to go.

Peace and contentment came when I became the Captain of my own fate; my own soul. No longer would I be the one who'd be thrown overboard or told to get off at the next stop, because I was at the helm; I was the Master; the Captain. It was *my* life.

Woman Find Thyself

Woman Find Thyself

PERSONAL CONSENT FORM

I, __*Cathy Upshire*__ , understand that everybody isn't going to like me, love me, accept me, embrace me, approve of me, affirm me, endorse me, value me, or see my worth and that I must give those who choose not to my "Full Consent".

I understand that if someone chooses not to do any of the above, I am not to convince them otherwise; not by my actions nor by my words, because to do so would result in the transfer of my own personal power.

I further understand that if someone has a negative opinion of me, it's okay, because everyone has a right to their own opinion, and equally so, I have a right to disagree. And I do exercise my right to disagree to its fullest degree.

I further understand that my failure to give my "Full Consent" regarding the above means that I dutifully and willfully become a major contributor to my own emotional pain and unhappiness.

[x] I confirm that I have read and fully understand the above.

__*Cathy Upshire*__   __12/24/YYYY__
Signature   Date

Woman Find Thyself

Power Boosters

Woman Find Thyself

Power Booster

It is a sad day
when a woman loses her power,
because when you lose your power,
you lose yourself.

Cathy Upshire

Woman Find Thyself

Power Booster

Emotional pain and woundedness is a byproduct of a powerless soul.

Cathy Upshire

Woman Find Thyself

Power Booster

Show me a woman
who has given away her power,
and I'll show you one who is
somewhere licking her wounds.

Woman *reclaim* your power;
heal thyself.

Cathy Upshire

Woman Find Thyself

Power Booster

People aren't necessarily causing your pain; not getting what you think you need from them is. Become whole and you will find that what you thought you needed, you won't need any more.

Cathy Upshire

Woman Find Thyself

Power Booster

Instead of trying to *be* yourself seek to be whole, because when you become whole the real you will emerge.

Cathy Upshire

Woman Find Thyself

Power Booster

Shame isn't about others' perception of you. It's about *your* perception of you and the fear that if they knew, they'd feel the same way *you* do about you.

Don't let what you've done or what was done to you taint your view *of* you.

Cathy Upshire

Woman Find Thyself

Power Booster

There's nothing worse than
changing yourself into a person
you think people are going to like
only to find they don't like her either.

Be yourself and let the
chips fall where they may.

Cathy Upshire

Woman Find Thyself

Power Booster

"I want people to love me for who I am."

Well who *are* you? If you're not being who you *really* are, we can't love you for WHO you are. So will the real you *please* stand up, so we can love *her*.

Cathy Upshire

WOMAN FIND THYSELF

Power Booster

When we accept and embrace who we are to the fullest we won't think to be anyone other than ourselves. It's only when our *own* identities come into question that we try to imitate or be someone other than who we really are.

Cathy Upshire

Woman Find Thyself

Power Booster

Rejection is a feeling,
not an event.

You can't *feel* rejected
if you're not trying to
be accepted.

Acceptance seeking is
Power leaking.

Cathy Upshire

WOMAN FIND THYSELF

Power Booster

Neediness and personal power are polar opposites and cannot coexist.

Cathy Upshire

Woman Find Thyself

Power Booster

When we give away our personal power, we make those we give it to more powerful than they already are. They have the personal power they came into the relationship with AND the power we give them; which makes for an unhealthy imbalance of power and the start of an unhealthy relationship. We don't want to give anyone any more power than they already have. If we do, they will abuse it, because power corrupts. Not always, but in the wrong hands it does.

Cathy Upshire

Woman Find Thyself

Power Booster

Wholeness is being able to be who you are without any concern for how it is going to be perceived.

Cathy Upshire

Woman Find Thyself

Power Booster

You can't look to those who hurt you to fix you anymore than you can look to a two year old to fix the piece of fine china he dropped and shatter into pieces. Some wounds require help beyond human endeavor; they require the *Hand of God*.

Cathy Upshire

Woman Find Thyself

Power Booster

What you're feeling on the inside has more to do with what's going on *with* you than what's going on *around* you.

Cathy Upshire

Woman Find Thyself

Power Booster

No—You Think She Is...

If you think she thinks she's superior to you, it's only because *you* think she is.

If you think she thinks she's better than you, it's only because *you* think she is.

If you think she thinks she's all that, it's only because *you* think she is.

If you think she thinks she's so cute, it's only because *you* think she is.

Our conclusions about what people are thinking of themselves reveals more about us and what *we* think of them

Cathy Upshire

Woman Find Thyself

Power Booster

If someone has a negative
opinion of you, it's okay.
People have a right
to their own opinion,
and you have a right
to disagree.

Question is...do you?

Cathy Upshire

Woman Find Thyself

Power Booster

You're not going to think to change you except you have concluded that something's wrong *with* you.

Cathy Upshire

Woman Find Thyself

Power Booster

The issue is not that others don't accept you. The issue is you don't accept yourself, because if you did, you wouldn't have an issue with those who don't.

Cathy Upshire

Woman Find Thyself

Power Booster

Better to be disliked for being who you are than being love for being who you aren't. If you live for the later, you're going to create a self-made prison for your authentic self, and it'll be just a matter of time before she'll start screaming to get out. Unfortunately, you may not have the courage to let her out, because everyone will have already fallen in love with the fictitious version of you. Be authentic from the start to urge those who won't like the "real" you to keep moving, so you'll have room for those who will.

Cathy Upshire

Woman Find Thyself

Power Booster

If you don't like someone else's personality, you're going to have to figure out what's going on inside of *you* that makes what they do bother you, because it really is *about* you. You can't expect someone to change who they are to accommodate you. Figure out what their personality reveals about *you* and then work on that. If you do that, you're going to find that the list of people you don't like will have shrunken considerably.

Cathy Upshire

Woman Find Thyself

Power Booster

To avoid making the same mistakes over and over again, ask yourself these important questions for each mistake you've made:

1. What was the mistake?
2. Who was impacted *by* the mistake?
3. What was lost as a result *of* the mistake?
4. What did I learn *from* the mistake?
5. Now that I know better, how could I have avoided *making* the mistake?

Starting today, live the life you would have had you known better.

Cathy Upshire

Woman Find Thyself

Power Booster

A scar is a permanent record of a lesson learned. Go back and review your scars when making future decisions so as to avoid the pitfalls that lead to their formation. Remember, before they were scars they were wounds. And whereas scars don't hurt wounds do.

Cathy Upshire

Woman Find Thyself

Power Booster

There is a lesson, a treasure, a connection; even a stepping stone reserved just for you on the other side of your fears and they are essential to your success. Burrow through them so that you can get to the thing that is divinely designed to change the trajectory of your life and propel you towards your destiny.

Cathy Upshire

Woman Find Thyself

Power Booster

You will find if you haven't already that your greatest teachers will be those who've caused you the most heartache and pain. And the lessons you'll learn from them will play a major role on your journey to wholeness.

Cathy Upshire

Woman Find Thyself

Power Booster

Wholeness is not needing anything from people they're neither willing nor prepared to give; whether it's acceptance, approval, affirmation, validation, honor, attention or love. The people who *really* matter are already providing it. You just have to come to the realization that what you already have is enough.

Cathy Upshire

Woman Find Thyself

Rhythm of My Heart

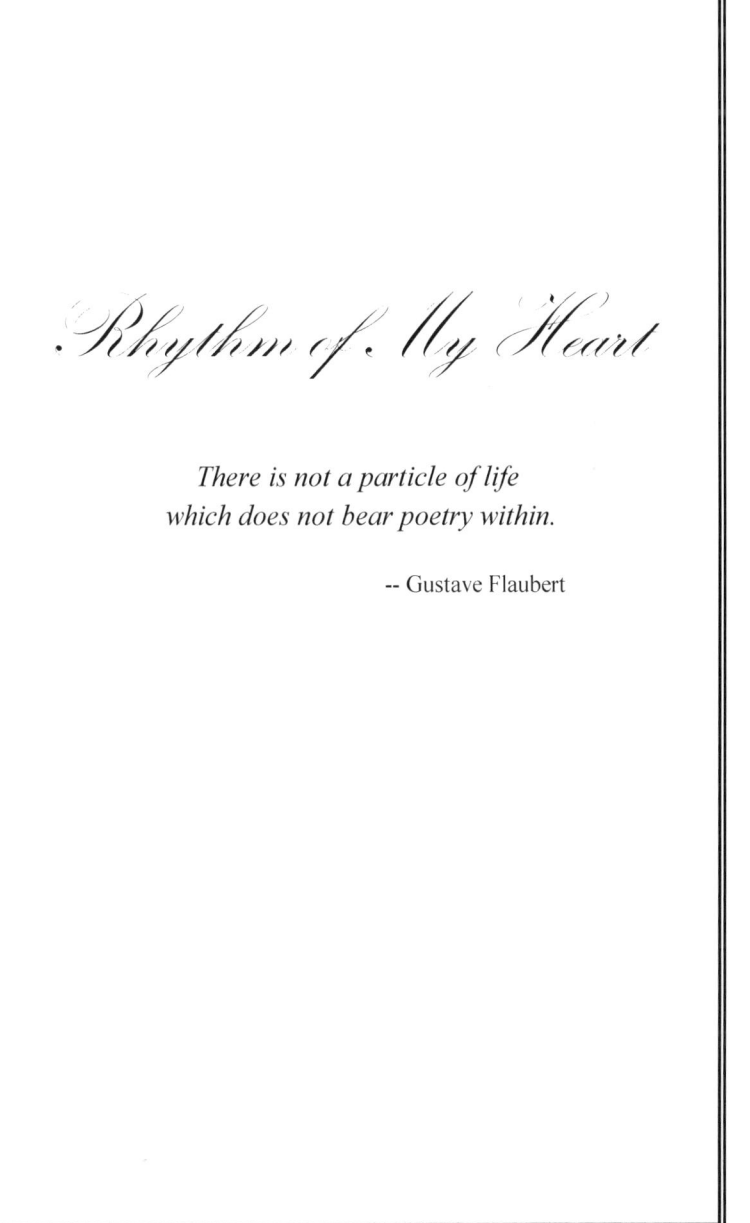

*There is not a particle of life
which does not bear poetry within.*

-- Gustave Flaubert

Woman Find Thyself

Why Am I Here?

Looking over my life and the choices I've made
    the streets I have traveled, the roads I have paved
        I struggle to reason behind every tear
            asking myself, "Why am I here?"

I've tried to move forward to no avail
    Something is hindering me. Is it from hell?
        When I think of tomorrow, I try not to fear
            I only ask, *"Why am I here?"*

Sometimes I look at those who are blessed
    and wonder how it is they escaped this mess
        Those are God's favorites, or so it appears
            and if that's not so, then why am *I* here?

Why am I in this desolate place
    Impoverished and destitute; oh what a disgrace
        A world of shattered hopes and dreams
            God forsaken or so it seems

I've tried to judge, but cannot tell
    Whether from heaven - whether from hell
        So I'll look deep inside where my spirit is still
            to search for the answer. Is this *God's* will?

Looking over my life, was it all just for naught
    the races I've run, the battles I've fought
        This just isn't fair! Oh dear, Oh dear
            Of all the people I know, "Why am *I* here?"

So God began to show me my plight
    For this I prayed both day and night
        Lord, didn't you hear me when first I prayed?
            The tears I've shed – the petitions I've made?

Yes, I heard each prayer you uttered
    But when I searched, your heart was cluttered
        With all kinds of things you wouldn't believe
            And if I had told you, you wouldn't have received

So I'm waiting until I have cleaned up the mess
    And when I am finished, I'll be ready to bless

                Cathy Upshire

Woman Find Thyself

Broken Wing

a raging fire
a burning flame
a hope to which I cling
to soar to heights
beyond the clouds
despite my broken wing.

Cathy Upshire

Woman Find Thyself

Had a Great Fall

The enemy stood accusing me
and guilt rolled in like a flood
When the Lord looked down
to see what I'd done
all he saw was his blood

Desperately I stood before my God
upon his name I called
He stretched forth his hands
and showed me new mercy
the day I had a great fall.

Cathy Upshire

Woman Find Thyself

And So I Hide

What can I say to myself on today
to help with what I'm feeling inside
Self-affirmations to increase my worth
aren't working at least in my eyes

So often I feel like damaged goods
Discarded and tossed aside
Left in a field where no one will tread
Not even a passerby

Who will see me, know me, love me
For the person I am inside
No one will love the person I am
No one *and so I hide*

Two lives I live – two stories I give
to keep the reproach at bay
because as soon as you learn the truth about me
you'll turn and walk away

Ashamed of what has happened to me
Ashamed of what I've done
Although I know they're not the same
To you they're all but one

A scarlet letter above my brow
Always considered a fool
Left without honor or social esteem
Marked by cultural rules

Ducking and dodging, hiding, covering
secrets, deceptions and lies
because you won't love me the way I am
I don't *and so I hide*

Cathy Upshire

Woman Find Thyself

Woman Find Thyself

I Lift Up My Head

I'm *not* what I did
and I'm *not* what they said
It's all in my past
So I lift up my head

I've moved from my place
of shame and instead
I *celebrate* my journey
and I lift up my head

Cathy Upshire

Woman Find Thyself

Hole in My Soul

Hole in my soul
I can't seem to fill
A hole in my soul
from wounds that won't heal

Hole in my soul
I can't seem to mend
It appeared out of nowhere
Don't know how or when

Hole in my soul
no joy in my song
I'm empty inside
and I know something's wrong

A hole in my soul
I keep trying to fill
but at the end of the day
I'm empty still

Cathy Upshire

Woman Find Thyself

I Thirst

Lead me to the streams where living waters run
the place where the weary are nursed
Help me, save me, heal me, fill me
Give me to drink Lord, **I Thirst**

Even the deer panteth for a drink
of life giving waters to live
So doeth my soul long for a drink
of the living water you give

Be with me Lord by the cool river's edge
dip me till I am immersed
Bathe me, wash me, cleanse me, flow through me
Give me to drink Lord, **I Thirst**

I Thirst to feel you, hear you, be near you
safe in your loving embrace
I Thirst for more and more of you
with every passing day

I Thirst for a heart like yours dear Lord
to serve my fellowman
I Thirst to be used by your power oh God
to fulfill my purpose, your plan

I come to you Lord in total surrender
and I'm willing to put you first
I stand before you empty, heart opened
Give me to drink Lord, **I Thirst**

Cathy Upshire

Woman Find Thyself

Woman Find Thyself

Looking for Love

Looking for love in all the wrong places
for the love I never got
looking for love and affirmation
in places were love was not

Couldn't let go of the way things were
hoping what was could be
finding it hard to let go of what was
although it was hurting me

Looking for love in all the wrong places
in hopes my prince would come
compromising myself to satisfy him
in hopes he'd be the one

Searched high and low to fill the hole
'til the light of truth I caught
and realized what I'd been searching for
was not in the places I thought

Surrendered my body wee hours of night
my husband I thought he'd be
I awoke to realize if I am to find love
it starts with loving me

Cathy Upshire

WOMAN FIND THYSELF

Woman Find Thyself

Can You See Me?

Can you see me? I'm right here in your face
It's kinda hard to miss me. I'm in the most obvious place
What color am I wearing? What color is my hair?
No one seems to notice or pretend they even care

Can you see me standing here? I can see you there just fine
Your eyes, hazel brown – your shoes the color of wine
I saw you when you entered the room. I saw you before you knew
I wonder if anyone noticed me the moment I came into view

Can you see me? Can you see me? Hey! What about you?
Touch my hand; feel my face – I wanna be sure you do
Can you see me? Can you? Can you hear my voice?
And if by chance you can't, was this a matter of choice?

Sorry ma'am, don't mean to bother, there's something I've just gotta know
It's just that sometimes I feel like I'm invisible
I know that isn't true. I know that couldn't be
I just don't understand why people aren't seeing me

When I looked in the mirror this morning, there was an image there
A woman of wisdom and grace – her countenance was fair
Look at me somebody! I'm worthy of at least a glance
For I am someone special, because I am in God's hands

Maybe you can't see me, because God has blinded your view
God has me in a secret place; grooming me for you
He's making me to be a blessing, a blessing yes indeed
An orchard of fruits and berries for others to come and feed

Can you see me? That's alright. One day it'll certainly be said
that I am exalted and highly favor; because I'll be eating the King's bread

Cathy Upshire

Woman Find Thyself

Prisoner to a Fortified Heart

On the inside looking out
Wondering what it is all about
Alienated – No one to hear
Barricaded by a wall of fear

I wasn't gonna let anyone else in
Vowing I'd *never* love again
Remember the city of Jericho
Well protected from friends or foe

Walls to fortify those within
Keeping intruders from getting in
Prepared to strike – prepared to defend
A deterrent to keep from being bruised again

But building walls is a tragedy
Only when built are you able to see
For this I know and for this thou art
A prisoner to a fortified heart

Protecting myself from those who would
I ended up doing more harm than good
For the walls I had built meticulously
Were the very walls that imprisoned me

I tried to escape to make my break
But the walls were too thick to penetrate
Not able to give, not able to love
What on earth was I thinking of

Silent screams echoed within
Desperately yearning to love again
So little by little with a steady pace
I dug my way out of that dreadful place

Get out! Get out! while you're able
Before it's too late to turn the tables
For this I know and for this thou art
A Prisoner to a *Fortified Heart*

Cathy Upshire

Woman Find Thyself

Face to Face

Face to face with my reflection
A woman encased in glass
Every time I look in my mirror
this woman reminds me of my past

She's bruised and marred, broken and scarred
and struggling with low-self esteem
And no one knows about the woman in my mirror
No, no one knows except me

Mirror, Mirror on the wall
Tell me what it is you see
You know me better than anyone else
What is *your* impression of me?

Well, you're faithful, honest, friendly, outgoing
and those are some of the good things I see
But I see a side you tried to hide
But you can't hide anything from me

You're bitter, resentful, selfish, judgmental
and, oh yeah, I've caught you gossiping too
Now I'm just telling you what it is I see
and the only person I see is you

Mirror, Mirror you must be mistaken
Because I don't see all that stuff you see
And I don't know who you're looking at from behind that glass
But the reflection you see ain't me

Now some people I love, but I just don't like
and sometimes I don't want to share
But I'm not like that lady with that blue dress on
Some of the things she does, I wouldn't *dare*

Now I have things to do and places to go
and I promise it won't take very long
And we're gonna talk about this again on tomorrow
because your impression of me was *wrong*

Cathy Upshire

Woman Find Thyself

WOMAN FIND THYSELF

The Imposter

Who's the woman in my mirror staring back at me
I see her every morning, but I don't like what I see
She wormed her way into my life – Oh, so gradually
And no one seemed to notice she's impersonating me

She seeks the approval of others; she tries to win their love
She tries to prove her worthiness. What is *she* thinking of?
She gave away my power and all my self-respect
My worst enemy she became; not this one, the other one, or that

She robbed me of my figure by gaining fifty pounds
By using food to comfort her when no one was around
The things I said I wouldn't do; I said I'd *never* allow
This woman *knew* just how I felt, but did them anyhow

How could I have let this happened or even let this be?
How could I have let this people pleaser masquerade as me?
She has my eyes, my nose, my mouth, my butt, my legs, my feet
But something's wrong and I'm *telling* you this woman isn't *me*

Help somebody! Help me now! Contact the CIA
I want this woman investigated, charged and taken away
Sentence her to *life* in prison and throw away the key
to ensure this woman will never *ever* show up somewhere as me

Cathy Upshire

Woman Find Thyself

What Would You Do If You Really Knew?

What would you do if you really, really knew
the person I'm not letting you see
And what would you think, what *would* you think
if I suddenly started acting like me

What would you say if you found out today
I'm not the person you knew
Would you grab your throat - gag and choke
and go, *"My God! Who are you?"*

What would you do if you really, really knew
I'm not who you think I should be
Would you still feel the same if I stopped playing these games
of Charade and Hide and Seek

See I play these games to shroud my shame
with a veil I use to cover me
Camouflaging my pain with a chameleon's array
a protective layer of coloring

If I took off the mask and suddenly revealed
the person that's hidden from view
Would you change your mind if you were to find
I'm really no different than you

I hurt, I cry, I weep, I ache
and sometimes I outright *sob!*
And trying to keep up this masquerade
is becoming quite a job

So I'm sorry if the person you got to know
was a fraud, a phony, a fake
But I'm tired of putting on this clandestine front
not another day of this can I take

So if you don't like the person I am
or the person I was created to be
Be gone, be gone, be on your way
because I've just *gotta* be me

Cathy Upshire

Woman Find Thyself

Woman Find Thyself

Beauty That Really Matters

You don't have to envy
the beauty of my skin
Beauty that really matters
is the beauty from within

You don't have to envy
the stride that's in my walk
or words fitly spoken
hen I open my mouth to talk

Don't be intimidated
when you're in my company
No big 'I's or little 'You's
Get to know me, you'll see

Although I may possess
the beauty of a queen
If ugly is on the inside
it doesn't mean a thing

You don't have to envy
this outer shell I'm in
beauty that *really* matters
is the beauty from within

Cathy Upshire

Woman Find Thyself

WOMAN FIND THYSELF

I Thought I Knew

I thought I knew the things that mattered
I thought would satisfy
But when I got just what I wanted
All *I* did was cry

I thought I knew which path to take
Though something said, *"Go Right!"*
But I thought the path to my left
Would lend a better plight

I thought I could do whatever I wanted
That things would turn out alright
But when I saw the state of my harvest
Boy did I see the light

I didn't think God kept his promises
Well the good ones, but not the bad
So when I didn't give him what was his
He took everything I had

I thought I had great wisdom and knowledge
and knew what worked or not
I thought I had it all figured out
Turns out? I didn't know *squat!*

Cathy Upshire

Woman Find Thyself

Woman Find Thyself

Starting Over

If I could do it all over again
and change the life I've lived
Go back and try and do it right
Oh *Lord,* what I'd give

If I could do it all over again
and given a second chance
to right the wrongs, I *promise* you
I'd do a different dance

If I knew then what I know now
I wouldn't have done what I did
If I had known it would turn out this way
I would've done better instead

So I'm going to live as if this is
the first day of my life
and use the insights I have gained
to go and do it right

I'll think about all the mistakes I've made
and think about what I've learned
I'll count up the cost of the things I've lost
to get everything I've earned

So today I'm reinvesting myself
and I won't even wait 'till noon
I'm starting over and this time around
I'll be singing a different tune

Cathy Upshire

Woman Find Thyself

What's in Your Box

Your life's a gift box beautifully rapped
its contents, your spirit, your soul
and most won't know what dwells inside
or the deep dark secrets it holds

Will the gift you bring make life better for me
or will it make it worse
Will I regret I accepted your gift
without examining it first

Does the gift you're holding in front of me
have humility stuffed inside
or will I be stunned to find that it's filled
with spite, malice and pride

Is there anger, bitterness, resentment, selfishness,
jealousy, control or hate?
I know you're eager to share your gift
But I'm sorry, I'd rather wait

I've learned my lesson, I've learned it well
from my not so distant past
the danger of letting the wrong people in
the danger of moving too fast

So before I accept the gift you bring
or even move one notch
Give me a moment to look inside
to see what's in your box

Cathy Upshire

Woman Find Thyself

Loving the Woman Within

Stop bringing up the things of old
    and reminding me of my sins
        The things that made me hate myself
            I'm not doing those things again

Yes, I gave myself to this one and that one
    and I did it again and again
        But this is now; that was then
            I'm loving the women within

Not understanding who I was
    or the merits of my worth
        Not realizing the value
            of the things I had from birth

Always last on the list
    and putting others first
        and feeling guilty when last I tried
            to buy a simple purse

So I'm gonna do something just for me
    and I'm not sharing it with you
        I feel I *deserve* to be first sometimes
            because I'm somebody *too*

I'm gonna love on myself
    cherish myself like a rare ruby or pearl
        And value the woman I am today
            I'm precious in all the world

I'm gonna take time to pamper myself
    and treat *me* like a queen
        And I don't expect to do anything less
            because my fiancé is the KING

Now I don't know what he saw in me
    but apparently something good
        So I'm gonna treat *myself* the way
            the bride of a King would

So girl, you better get up from there
    and do something with your hair
        Buy a new dress, a new pair of shoes
            an extreme makeover if you dare

Now, some of you may not understand
    and to some it might be a sin
        But a girl's gotta do what a girl's gotta do
            'cause I'm *Loving the Woman Within*

Cathy Upshire

Woman Find Thyself

WOMAN FIND THYSELF

Authentic Woman

I *am* woman
I *am* me
I *am* living
Authentically!

Cathy Upshire

Woman Find Thyself

Satisfied

I went in broken, but I came out whole
I went in timid, but now I'm bold
I went in wounded, but now I'm healed
I went in hungry, but now I'm filled
I went in thirsty, but all things aside
I came out rejoicing, I'm *Satisfied!*

Cathy Upshire

Woman Find Thyself

ABOUT THE AUTHOR

I'm Cathy Upshire; a writer, poet, speaker, minister and wholeness coach. I'm also a former crisis advocate for women coming out of violent relationships, and a former medical crisis advocate for victims of sexual assault. As I've gotten older I've moved from living a more ambition driven life to living a more purpose driven life. This shift in my focus has given me a clearer sense of my purpose and that is to help women who've lost their sense of identity and power to not only reclaim it so that they can live their lives with dignity and resolve, but to help them break free from the clenching jaws of their past."

I've also written three other books; *Evolution of a Woman* available on Amazon.com and Barnes & Noble.com, an inspirational piece, *"Flying at High Altitudes (You're Not Living if You're Not Loving)"* and a literary narrative memoir, *"Let Go of the Branch (Trusting God in a Freefall)."* Both are soon to be released.

I am also the mother of three adult children
(Andre, Quincy and Aja)
who are all the loves of her life.

Woman Find Thyself

Made in the USA
Columbia, SC
28 March 2018